Catherine Brennand's
France

Copyright © Mark Brennand 2010

First published in 2010 by Newbridge Press,
Coign Chambers, 1 Newbridge Avenue, WV6 0LW

ISBN 13: 978-0-9563499-1-0

Printed in the UK by Information Press, Oxford

For more information about Catherine Brennand go to www.catherinebrennand.co.uk

CONTENTS

FOREWORD

From the time Catherine was elected to the Royal Institute of Painters in Water Colours, she was an enthusiastic member. Her paintings were first selected and shown at an RI exhibition at the Mall Galleries in 1991, when she entered work as a young painter and was awarded the Winsor & Newton Young Artists Award. A year later she was elected a member and contributed pictures over the next fourteen years.

Her paintings were mainly of architectural subjects, selected from the many locations she visited, making notes and photographing the details and the texture of buildings in close up and introducing her own individual colour scheme in her interpretation of the subject.

Over time her paintings were constantly in demand by gallery owners visiting our exhibition who were keen to show and sell her work.

For a time she was a member of the RI Council, always putting forward ideas and thoughts on how we could further promote the RI for future events. An opportunity occurred with an exhibition in the Midlands – at the Lichfield Festival – with an invited RI exhibition in the Chapter House of Lichfield Cathedral. Catherine, not living too far away, agreed to plan and supervise the hanging of the all the members' paintings. This she did very successfully.

The theme of this book – containing as it does many paintings of buildings in the decorative style of French architecture – demonstrates how well the subjects were suited to her style and how they had a profound influence on her future work. It is also interesting to note the legacy of her ideas of close up details and how it has influenced other artists, giving them inspiration in their selected subjects, not only of buildings but on other themes.

Above all this book demonstrates Catherine's versatility as an artist.

Ronald Maddox
President Royal Institute of
Painters in Water Colours

INTRODUCTION

There is a moment in the film Four Weddings and a Funeral when the character played by James Fleet meets the girl of his dreams and under his breath utters the words "Lightning bolt city".

It sounds rather trite but on first meeting Catherine I experienced the same. We were at a Halloween Party and from the word go just clicked. What attracted me, apart from her physical beauty, was how bright yet uncomplicated she appeared.

Within six weeks we were notionally living together and by the summer of the following year were still enjoying one another's company and finding plenty to talk about. We therefore decided to put our compatibility to the litmus test of a three week holiday in France.

Thus in August 1987, we headed south to the Mediterranean resort of Palavas, close to Montpellier, a city whose elegance had made such an impact on me ten years previously. When not relaxing on the beach we travelled to Aigues-Mortes, Montpellier, Nîmes, the Pont du Gard and Sète, before heading across country to Le Castellet, from where Marseille, Cassis and Sanary were all visited. Our three week sojourn ended in La Cavallier, a base from which to visit St Tropez and Cannes. Far from drying up, the trip generated even more to talk about and convinced me that Catherine was someone to whom I could wholeheartedly commit.

At the time she was working as a Market Analyst for Tarmac Building Materials whose headquarters were in Wolverhampton. Her passion for the products the firm made was both unusual and disarming and stemmed from her first job as a technical graphic artist for a concrete block manufacturer. Her role had been to create marketing literature to demonstrate the ways in which the company's blocks could be used. To me a concrete block was just a concrete block; grey, angular and rather bland. To her, an object of beauty and it was this passion that fostered a fascination with buildings and architecture. But, bar a substantial portfolio of technical drawings, there were few outward signs of the nascent artist.

That soon changed when, within a month of returning from France, she presented me with a painting of a building in Le Castellet. Its bright colours and almost abstract composition enthralled me and after a brief pause I said, "Heh – you could make a living at this".

It was a light bulb moment. From that point on Catherine began to devote her every spare moment to painting, a bedroom at home becoming her studio. But, despite all her effort, it would take four years before she found a style which was both sufficiently distinctive and to a standard that could hold its own in an exhibition. At which point fate played its hand.

Catherine's close college friend, Sarah, had recently married Peter Dawson. He was Art Advisor to Hertford County Council and more significantly, a member of the Royal Institute of Painters in Water Colours, Britain's premier Watercolour Society. He had seen Catherine's work and encouraged her to submit work to the Institute's Annual Exhibition which, as it had always done since its inception in 1846, welcomed entries from non members. In 1991 her piece, "Façade, Aix-en-Provence" was accepted into the exhibition and more importantly, went on to win the Winsor and Newton Young Painter of the Year Award. Greatly encouraged, the following year Catherine submitted six pieces, all of which were accepted. With the additional support of Leo McDowell, another prominent RI member, she was elected as a full member of the Institute.

It's hard to underestimate the lift that this provided, both to her confidence and reputation, as a new world of galleries eager to sell her work opened up. Within five years she was doing sufficiently well to leave her job at Tarmac to paint full time. From that point on, until her death from breast cancer in 2006, she earned a living solely from her art.

Artists are not unusual in concentrating on one particular subject. For Catherine that subject was buildings. In a 1998 interview for Artist Magazine she said *"Focusing on an individual subject isn't necessarily a bad thing. I cannot imagine ever becoming bored with painting buildings. There are so many architectural styles and every place has its own flavour. I am particularly interested in the use of light and shadows and because of that the building surface is constantly changing. A good light can make the most mundane of buildings look exciting"*. She would often find inspiration from the upper storeys and by skewing the perspective shifted the subject from the merely mundane into a thing of distinctive beauty.

During her short career she completed almost 900 works of buildings in Britain, France, Italy, Greece, Israel, the USA and Malta. All were assiduously recorded with a photograph, a completion date and a note of the dimensions. It is this record that has provided me with the means to publish this book.

With so much to choose from, why have I chosen to start with France?

For the two of us the years from 1987 to 1996 were a gilded period; one in which, free from parental responsibilities, we would invariably travel to France for our annual summer holiday. And it was during these holidays that Catherine drew much of the early inspiration for her work in the towns and cities of the Mediterranean south. A good deal of our time was spent wandering around narrow streets and squares, observing shuttered windows, doorways, peeling plaster and pan tiled roofs. This research would evolve into the defining structure of our holidays, Catherine clicking away on her camera all the while thinking about suitable subjects to paint. Anything further from work I have yet to find, but that is what it was. Once back home the paintings would soon start to appear allowing us to relive the holiday.

It was therefore France that first inspired her and France that set the template for how we would spend so much of our subsequent life together, in which holidays and the shared interest in architecture, photography and art played such a major part.

David Hockney, an artist whose work Catherine much admired, once said; "It is good advice to believe only what an artist does, rather than what he says about his work."

Heeding those words I will end here and leave you free to enjoy her work.

Mark Brennand
July 2010, Wolverhampton

AIX-EN-PROVENCE

Brennan

A I X - E N - P R O V E N C E

Quite why Aix-en-Provence was omitted from our first trip to the South of France in 1987 is a mystery.

Aix is one of *those* cities — tree lined boulevards, narrow streets, beautiful old doorways and enchanting squares embracing al fresco cafes and restaurants. All of it charming and inducing of envy such that, once home, we resolve to emigrate as soon as the chance presents itself.

For Catherine Aix opened her eyes to the possibilities offered by tall shuttered buildings, stuccoed walls, peeling plaster all set within the context of Mediterranean sunlight.

The Red Cross Hospital,
Aix-en-Provence
(1989)

*Façade,
Aix-en-
Provence.*

(1990)

Corner of a street,
Aix-en-Provence.
(1990)

Doorway with Stone Vases,
Aix-en-Provence.
(1996)

Ornate Doorway in Gold & Blue,
Aix-en-Provence.
(1996)

Blue Shutters, Place de Palmiers,
Aix-en-Provence.
(1996)

*Green Lantern,
Aix-en-Provence.*
(1996)

*Three Stone Faces,
Aix-en-Provence.*
(1996)

Statue on Corner of Rue Thiers, Aix-en-Provence.
(1996)

Number 2 Place des Palmiers, Aix-en-Provence.
(1996)

Corner of Rue Aude,
Aix-en-Provence.
(1996)

Corner of a
courtyard,
Aix-en-Provence.
(1996)

Boutiques on Cours Mirabeau, Aix-en-Provence.
(1996)

Three Stone Faces at Number 10, Aix-en-Provence.
(1996)

Lantern at Number 10, Aix-en-Provence.
(1996)

*Gold Corinthian
Columns, Cours
Mirabeau,
Aix-en-Provence.*
(1996)

*Green Shutters at
No 9, Aix-en-Provence.*
(1996)

*Green Shutters at
No 7, Aix-en-Provence.*
(1996)

Ornate Doorway, Place des Palmiers, Aix-en-Provence.

(1996)

No 21, Cours Mirabeau,
Aix-en-Provence.

(1996)

Stone Vases at No 40,
Aix-en-Provence.

(1996)

Green Door at No 18,
Aix-en-Provence.

(1996)

Rue Thiers, Aix-en-Provence.
(1996)

La Boutique Française, Aix-en-Provence.
(1996)

The Cathedral,
Aix-en-Provence.

(1996)

Rue Sallier,
Aix-en-Provence.

(1996)

*Number 15,
Aix-en-Provence.*

(1996)

*Green Shutters at Rue Aude,
Aix-en-Provence.*

(1996)

Gate with Lion's Head,
Aix-en-Provence.

(1997)

Furled Tricolore, Aix-en-Provence.

(1997)

*Crimson Wall, Rue
Sallier, Aix-en-Provence.*

(1997)

*Number 13,
Aix-en-Provence.*

(1997)

The Watchmaker's House,
Aix-en-Provence.

(1997)

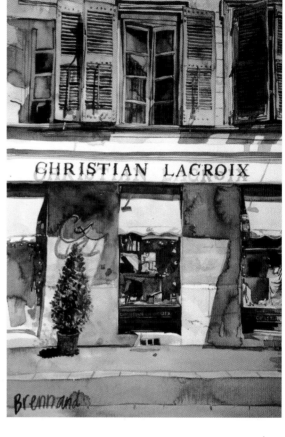

*The Grand Hotel,
Aix-en-Provence.*

(1997).
Reproduced by
kind permission of
Charles Gothard

The Grand Hotel
Aix - en - Provence
(Cours Mirabeau)

36 x 54 cm
June 1997
commission for
charles Gothard

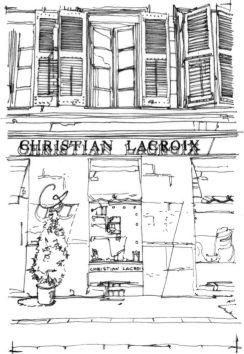

*Christian Lacroix,
Aix-en-Provence.*

(1997)

| Corner Rue Thiers,
| Aix-en-Provence.

(1998)

| Balconies,
| Aix-en-Provence.

(1998)

Ornate Balcony, Cours Mirabeau,
Aix-en-Provence.

(2003)

Société Générale, 16 Cours Mirabeau,
Aix-en-Provence.

(2003)

Ornate Door, 14 Cours
Mirabeau, Aix-en-Provence.

(2003)

Green Door, Cours Mirabeau,
Aix-en-Provence.

(2003)

Biblioteque pour tous, 19 Rue Cardinale, Aix-en-Provence.

(2004)

Green Door & Shutters at No 27, Aix-en-Provence.

(2004)

Christian Lacroix,
Aix-en-Provence.

(2004)

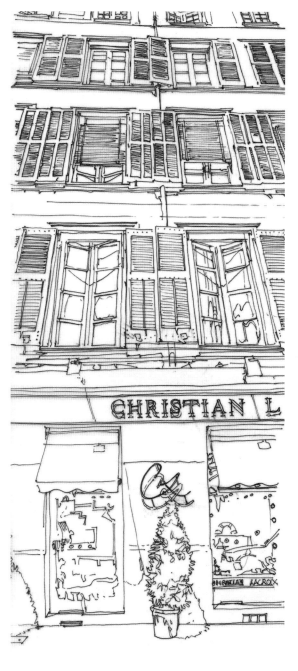

Red Geraniums at No 33,
Aix-en-Provence.

(2004)

Monoprix,
Aix-en-Provence.

(2004)

Monoprix
Aix-en-Provence

20·5cm
20·5cm

w/c & collage

Jan 2004

Geraniums on a balcony,
Aix-en-Provence.

(2004)

10·3cm X 2↑ X 88%
= 19·4cm x 45cm

X200% X 135% = 28cm wide
i. l-d broccolini at N° 35. Aix én P. (Jan 04)

Arched Doorway at No 35,
Aix-en-Provence.

(2004)

Brennand

*La Table Aixoise
Restaurant,
Aix-en-Provence.*

(2004)

Montpellier

MONTPELLIER

There can be few more civilising spaces than Montpellier's Place de la Comédie. At one end sits the elegant 19th century Opera House fronted by the Fontaine de Trois Grace and surrounded on all sides by buzzing cafes. And leading off this space is a labyrinth of narrow streets and chic shops all frequented by the city's young and vibrant student population.

We first went together in 1987, and that was followed by many memorable visits.

Salle Molière,
Montpellier.

(1996)

Terracotta Pots outside the
Montpellier Chamber of Commerce.

(1995)

Hotel du Palais, Montpellier.
(1993)

Green Shutters, Montpellier.
(1996)

Green Balconies, Montpellier.
(1996)

Ornate balcony, Montpellier.
(1997)

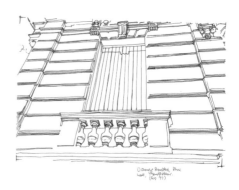

Orange Shutters, Blue Wall, Montpellier.

(1997)

*Evening Light,
Montpellier.*

(1997)

*Console with Roaring
Lion's Head,
Montpellier.*

(1997)

*Ironwork Balcony,
Montpellier.*

(1997)

Rue du 4 Septembre, Montpellier.
(1997)

Ironwork Balcony at No 4, Montpellier.
(1998)

*Reflection of the Gaumont, Place
de la Comédie, Montpellier.*

(2004)

*Banque NSMD, Rue Foch,
Montpellier.*

(2004)

10·5 x 24·5 x (200%) = 21 x 49   x (143%) = 30 x 70
                         cm   cm   cm   cm
                              or   x (110%) = 23 x 54
                                             cm   cm

The Corner of Rue Foch and Rue D'Albisson, Montpellier.

(2004)

*Pâtisserie Valgalier,
Rue du Faubourg St
Jaumes, Montpellier.*

(2004)

Arles

ARLES

Despite the romantic association with Vincent Van Gogh, it would take us four trips to the South of France before we finally paid a visit to Arles. This might be on account of its somewhat isolated position, on the banks of the River Rhône. Its Amphitheatre is one of the best preserved Roman monuments in Provence and Catherine's line drawing and subsequent painting capture, fully, its commanding presence. Here too saw her first experiment with compositions verging on the abstract.

Place du Forum, Arles.
(1994)

Ivy on a house in Arles.
(1994)

Hotel du Forum,
Arles.

(1994)

Place du Forum,
Arles.

(1994)

*Gold Wall, Rond Point
des Arènes, Arles.*
(1997)

Blue Wall, Arles

(1997)

Flags on the Rue de la Calade, Arles.

(1997)

*Arches of the
Amphitheatre at Arles.*
(1997)

House at No 21,
Arles.

(1998)

Ornate Balcony in blue and gold,
Arles.

(1998)

Tricolore at Arles Town Hall.
(1998)

Ornate Doorway in gold and green, Arles.
(1998)

Tiny window and ornate arch, Arles.
(1998)

Bastille Day,
Arles.

(1999)

European Flags,
Arles.

(1999)

Brennand

36cm
65cm

Villa Romana
Arles

water colour & tissue collage

June
2004

AIGUES-MORTES

A I G U E S - M O R T E S

Guide books can be rather disparaging about Aigues-Mortes whose historic association with the Crusades has, they claim "...been submerged by tat. Worth visiting more for the effect of the ensemble, than the tacky shops within."

On our numerous visits this was not a view that prevailed, perhaps explained by Catherine's view "Street level is often very ordinary, so I tend to look up quite a lot".

No 35,
Aigues-Mortes.

(1996)

No 41,
Aigues-Mortes.

(1996)

Hotel de Ville,
Aigues-Mortes.

(1996)

*Blue Shutters,
Aigues-Mortes.*
(1997)

68

Church, Aigues Mortes, the Camargue   7th
In the twelth century Louis XI set off for the First Crusade from Aigues Mortes
      eleventh
         ?

No 25 Aigues-Mortes.
(1997)

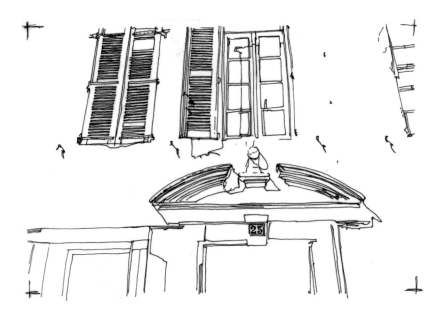

Ornate Balcony, Aigues-Mortes.
(1998)

Balcony at No 23, Aigues-Mortes.
(2004)

CENTRAL & NORTHERN FRAN

CENTRAL & NORTHERN FRANCE

Like many Northern Europeans we were not alone in our desire to get to the sun as quickly as possible. The result ; Central and Northern France became an area to pass through, all too rapidly, on our way to the south.

There were, however, some memorable stopovers. Brioude, to the south of Clermont-Ferrand, which provided the subject for Catherine's early studies of doors. Entraygues-sur-Truyère, in the Massif Central, where she painted the modest tanner's house over-looking the River Truyère — it would become the logo on her stationery. And at the opposite end of the social scale the implausible opulence of the Chateau at Chantilly.

Tanner's Houses,
Entraygues sur Truyère,
Massif Central
(1987)

Street in Brioude, Central
France.
(1990)

Doors in Brioude, Central France.
(1990)

Door at No 21, Nuits-St-Georges, Borgogne.

(1993)

Leaping Goat Statue, Chantilly Chateau.

(1995)

Bronze Head,
Chantilly Chateau.
(1995)

Green Door at Number 1,
Chantilly.
(1995)

Le Monde.
(1999)

The Weather Forecast, France.
(1999)

LANGUEDOC & ROUSSILLON

LANGUEDOC & ROUSSILLON

In the summer of 1978, for what was to be my last family holiday my parents rented a shabby apartment in the no-frills seaside resort of Carnon. Not for us the bright lights of the Cote D'Azur. Yet what it lacked in glamour it made up for in substance since from Carnon we could visit the historic Roman towns of Nîmes, Montpellier and Sète. That first visit set the foundation for a love affair with the area one that I was keen to present to Catherine.

The Tricolore, Hotel de Ville, Béziers.
(1999)

La Semaine Fantastique,
Béziers.

(1999)

*Palais Nîmes,
Reflection of the
Amphitheatre,
Nîmes.*

(2004)

*La Café Bourse,
Nîmes*

(2004)

*Reflection of the
Maison Carrée, Nîmes.*
(2004)

·Agde·

PROVENCE & COTE D'AZUR

PROVENCE & COTE D'AZUR

Neither Catherine nor I were particularly attracted to the glamour of the Cote D'Azur perceiving it to be the somewhat superficial preserve of the rich and famous and, as a consequence, overly crowded. We did however spend a day touring its length and on a couple of occasions visited Cannes and St Tropez, the latter proving to be refreshingly unspoilt.

It is of course a large and diverse area, Marseille and Grasse offering an antidote to the glitz of the former.

Yellow Door, Le Castellet, Provence.
(1987)

*Looking down a street in
St Tropez.*

(1989)

A street in Cyreste, Provence.
(1990)

Backstreets of Marseille.
(1990)

Villa St Pierre, Cannes, Cote D'Azur.
(1991)

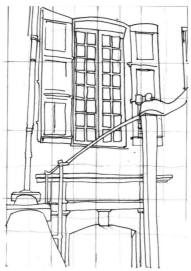

The Marine Museum II, Orange and Blue, Grasse, Cote D'Azur.
(1993)

Menton Church
(1993)

Cercle Fragonard, Grasse.
(1993)

No 37, Avignon Door.
(1993)

*Plane Tree, Cercle
Fragonard, Grasse.*
(1993)

*No 92, Fréjus Door,
Cote D'Azur.*
(1993)

*Bunting in Fréjus,
Cote D'Azur.*

(1993)

*Palm Tree, Sanary,
Cote D'Azur.*

(1993)

Saint in a Niche, Avignon.
(1993)

Door at No 24, Fayence,
Gulf D'Estoril.
(1993)

Gold Façade, Avignon.
(1994)

Ornamental Ironwork,
Avignon.
(1994)

*Classical Style
Window, Orange.*

(1996)

*Blue shutters, gold wall,
Orange.*

(1996)

Crimson Shutters, Orange.
(1997)

Stes-Marie-de-la-Mer, Camargue.
(1997)

La Mirande, Avignon.
(1997)

Red curtain, Red geraniums, Fréjus.
(1998)

LA CORSE

La Corse

On our first visit to Corsica in 1990 we were taken by the island's air of gentle decay, predicated on a determination by the Corsicans to prevent their beloved homeland from being submerged under modern development.

The see sawing influence of Italy and France is clearly evident in the architecture and provided ample material for Catherine's distinctive studies.

*Two wooden doors,
Bonifacio, La Corse.*

(1997)

*Crumbling Steps,
Bonifacio, La Corse.*
(1997)

*Number 10,
Bonifacio, La Corse.*
(1997)

Balconies in the Rue
Bonaparte, Ajaccio, La Corse.
(1997)

*Grey Shutters,
Bastia, La Corse.*

(1998)

*Green Shutters, Bastia,
La Corse.*

(1998)

Tricolore, Hotel de Ville,
Bastia, La Corse.

(1998)

The Corsican Flag, the French Tricolore and the
European Flag, the airport Ajaccio, La Corse.

(1999)

PARIS

PARIS

By August 1999 our second son Tom had reached the ripe old age of 15 months. With typical generosity Catherine's parents asked whether they could look after the boys whilst we could enjoy a long weekend break. Answering before they could withdraw the offer, we arranged to visit Paris.

Armed with a couple of walks from our close friend John Lenanton – who knew Paris intimately – over the ensuing three days we literally walked ourselves into the ground. But by the end Catherine had enough material to last her a lifetime, particularly of shops, a subject that would become such a feature in her later paintings of London.

Notre Dame, Paris.
(1999)

Fauchon, Place de la Madeleine, Paris.
(1999).

Christofle, Place de la Vendôme, Paris.
(1999).

Hediard, Place de la Madeine, Paris.
(1999).

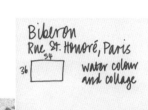

Biberon
Rue St. Honoré, Paris
36 [54]   water colour
and collage

for LBG. "RI 2000 exhibition"

| Biberon, Rue St Honoré, Paris.
(1999).

Cartier, Place de la Vendôme, Paris.
(1999).

Cristal Lalique, Rue de Rivoli,
Paris.

(1999)

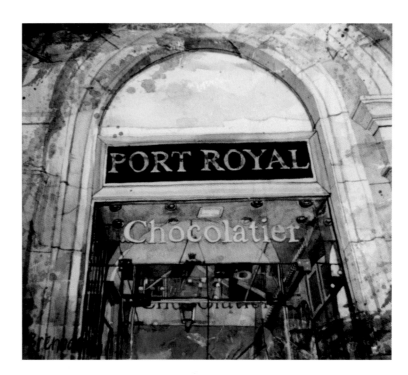

Port Royal Chocolatier,
Rue de Rivoli, Paris.
(2000)

Chanel, Rue Royale, Paris.
(2000)

Institut de Beauté Guerlain,
Champs Elysées, Paris.

(1999)

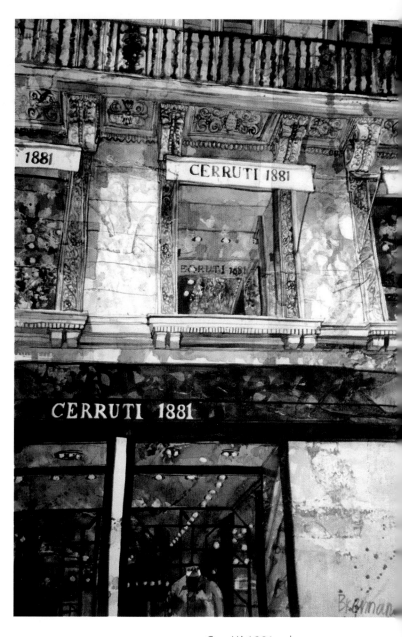

Cerutti 1881,
Rue Royale, Paris.

(2000)

Le Gastelier Salon de Thé,
Montmartre, Paris.
(2000)

Arcades des Champs
Elysées, Paris
(2000)

Geleries Felix Haloux,
Ile St Louis, Paris.

(2000)

Boulangerie St Louis,
Ile St Louis, Paris.

(2000)

*Boulangerie
L. Chevalier
Montmartre,
Paris.*

(2000)

2.1.5cm x 200% = 43cm x 160% = 69cm

*Vins Fins Fromages,
Rue Tardieu, Montmartre.
Paris*
34cm
to
cm

watercolour

February 2000

*Vins Fins –
Fromages,
Rue Tardieu,
Montmartre.*

(2000)

Les Deux Margots,
St Germain des Prés,
Paris.

(2000)

Le Petit Zinc Restaurant,
St Germain des Prés, Paris.

(2000)

Café de Flore,
St Germain des Prés, Paris.

(2000)

Evening light at Fauchon,
Place de la Madeleine, Paris.

(2000)

Restaurant Le Consulat,
Montmartre, Paris.
(2000)

Guerlain, Rue Tronchet, Paris.
(2000)

Devernois,
Rue Tronchet,
Paris.

(2000)

Gucci, Place de Vendôme,
Paris.

(2000)

Epicerie de la Tour,
Tour Eiffel, Paris.

(2000)

Jo Goldenberg Delicatessen, Rue
Ferdinand Duval, Le Marais, Paris.

(2000)

*Boucheron, Place
Vendôme, Paris.*
(2000)

*Red Crates outside Epicerie de la
Tour, Eiffel Tower, Paris.*
(2000)

The Ritz, Place Vendôme, Paris.
(2000)

Cartier, Place Vendôme, Paris.
(2000)

Hotel Vendôme, Place Vendôme, Paris
(2000)

Three Stone Heads. Bulgari, Place Vendôme, Paris.
(2000)

Biberon & Fils, 334
Rue St Honoré, Paris.

(2000)

*Shadow of Street
Lamp, Cristal Lalique,
Rue de Rivoli, Paris.*
(2000)

*Salon de Thé,
Du Lys d'Argent,
Ile St Louis, Paris.*
(2000)

Conifers outside Cristofle,
Place Vendôme, Paris.
(2000)

Aux Tortues, Boulangerie,
Rue Tronchet, Paris.
(2000)

Evening Light, Institut de Beauté Guerlain, Champs Elysées, Paris.
(2000)

Gold Lantern, Cristal Lalique, Rue de Rivoli, Paris.
(2000)

Devernois, Rue Tronchet, Paris.
(2000)

Guerlain Rue Tronchet, Paris.
(2000)

*Marie Curie's House, 36 Quai
D'Orléans, Ile St Louis, Paris.*

(2001)

*Chopin's House (Chaumet)
12 Place Vendôme, Paris.*

(2001)

Looking up at Cartier,
Place Vendôme, Paris.
(2001)

Pâtisserie Capucines, Rue du Sèze, L'Opéra, Paris.
(2001)

Café de la Paix, Place L'Opéra, Paris.
(2001)

Ministère de la Justice, Place Vendôme, Paris.
(2001)

Marionnaud, Rue des Maturins, Paris.
(2001)

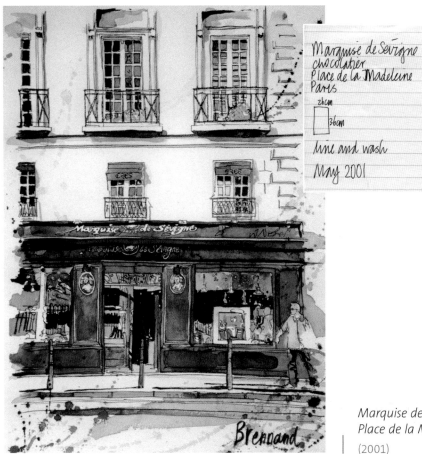

Marquise de Sevigne
chocolatier
Place de la Madeleine
Paris

26cm

36cm

line and wash

May 2001

*Marquise de Sevigne Chocolatier,
Place de la Madeleine, Paris.*

(2001)

*Café Madeleine, Place de la
Madeleine, Paris.*

(2001)

Plane tree outside Guerlain,
Champs Elysées, Paris.
(2001)

Le Tardieu Café,
Montmartre, Paris.
(2002)

Le Gastelier, Salon de Thé,
Montmartre, Paris.

(2002)

Quai d'Orléans,
Ile de Paris, Paris.

(2002)

SCRAPBOOK AND DIARY NOTES

1987

Various Locations – South of France

Saturday 23rd August to Saturday 12th September.

Itinerary

23rd August – Ferry sailing from Portsmouth to Caen (Ouistreham). Drive to Ecommoy south of Le Mans. Overnight stay at local campsite.

24th August – Ecommoy to Aurillac. Overnight stay at Terrain Camping de L'Ombrade.

25th – August – Aurillac to Palavas (Beach front town west of La Grande Motte).

25th – 30th August – Palavas Camping, Palavas Les Flots. Whilst here visits to: Sète, La Grande Motte, Montpellier, Aigues Morte, Pont du Gard, Nîmes.

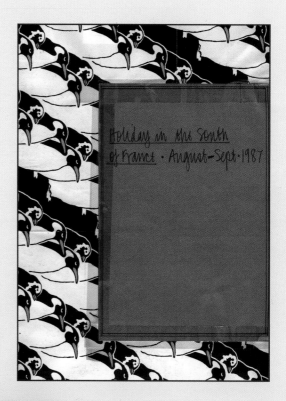

Aigues-Mortes

Tanner's House,
Entraygues

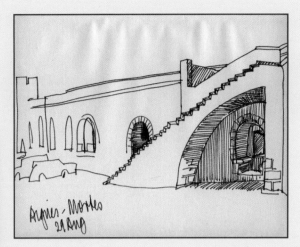

Aigues-Mortes
29 Aug

What to do and see...

go early – becomes packed.

1: Aigues-Mortes – port in the crusades

2: Le Grau-du-Roi – fishing, smaller and prettier than Sète

3: Port-Camargue – "little Venice"

4: Saint Marie de la Mere – the Camargue for lunch. Church worth a visit

5: St Gilles – old place (for wine) or lunch

6: Nîmes – big, busy, but lovely city with much division Roman ruins

---

C17 into private mansion [10F. park only 5F]
View from terrace – Cévennes, Languedoc Plain, Aigues-Mortes, Camargue.

Pont du Gard: aqueduct : Agrippa 19 BC : the bridge : the water channel (specus) is carried 130ft high over the river valley. Laid without mortar. blocks of 6 tons. Tour : about 1 hour . near Castillon village spot on Gardon back in front of entrance to St-Privat Château (500m above the aqueduct) outstanding view. Can walk across top or middle level.

closed mondays
on the left coming out of St. Laurent-d'Aigouze and D265 at the main crossroads in Marseillargues. beyond bridge dirt track on right

---

Aigues-Mortes

13C golden stone ramparts originally surrounded by a moat developed in 1240 by Louis IX preparing to set on a crusade to liberate Jerusalem Constance Tower, he built to defend the harbour : bread oven, chapel, knights Hall Prison for politically detainees and Templar barons and Huguenots. Climb watch tower for panoramic view. Ramparts built between 1272 and 1300. Towers in order of approach Salt (Sel) Wick Tower (Tour de la Mèche) the Villeneuve, the Magazine (Poudrière) and the Burgundians Tower ← name from the 100 yrs War (1418) from defending Burgundians surprised and slaughtered and salted by Armagnacs.

Excursions: Midi Salt Marshes
Teillan Castle : 8 miles NE by D979. transformed in the middle ages to a priory

---

Sts-Maries-de-la-Mer

legendary origin – gypsies. Pilgrimage centre . 12C Romanesque construction sights : church

St. Gilles : St Giles and the hind. legend Church : 12C Abbey. eastern gateway to the Camargue.

Nîmes Amphitheatre. Maison Carrée – temple built in 1BC Diana's Temple, Tour Magne) inclusive ticket 10F

31st August – Palavas to Le Beausset. Stay at Domaine de la Bergerie near to the Paul Ricard Circuit where Catherine's parents had bought a mobile home.

31st August – 4th September – Domaine de la Bergerie. Whilst here visits to: Bandol, Le Castellet, Cassis and La Ciotat.

4th September – Le Beausset to Cavalier Sur Mer.

4th – 8th September – Cavalier Sur Mer Campsite. Whilst here visit to St Tropez.

9th September – Cavalier Sur Mer to Roanne. Overnight stay at Camping Municipal, Roanne.

10th September – Roanne to Blois. Overnight stay at Lac du Loire, Blois.

11th September – Blois to Benouville near Ouistreham. Overnight stay at Camping Les Hautes Coutures, Benouville.

12th Ferry sailing from Ouistreham to Portsmouth.

Montpellier – Place de la Comédie

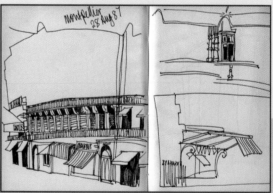

Cassis

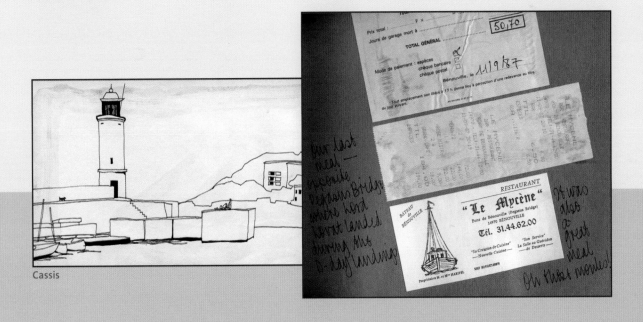

Church
La Ciotat
3rd Sept
1987

Cassis 2nd September 1987

Cassis

Our last meal — probable Pegasus Bridge where hard boat landed during the D-day landing

RESTAURANT
"Le Mycène"
Pont de Bénouville (Pegasus Bridge)
14970 BÉNOUVILLE
Tél. 31.44.62.00

It was also a great meal. Oh that moules!

1989

HOLIDAY IN THE SOUTH OF FRANCE JUNE 1989

Le Beausset, South of France

Saturday 24th June – Saturday 8th July.

Itinerary

24th June – Overnight ferry sailing from Portsmouth to Caen (Ouistreham). Drive from Caen to Brioude just south of Clermont Ferrand. Overnight stay at the Hotel Moderne.

25th June – Brioude to Le Beausset. Domaine de la Bergerie, Le Beausset.

26th June – 5th July – Domaine de la Bergerie. Whilst here visits to: Sanary, La Cardière D'Azur, Le Castellet, Le Beausset, Bandol, Marseilles, St Anne d'Evenos, Aix-en-Provence, Cassis, Cyreste and Hyères.

6th July – Le Beausset to Beaune. Overnight stay at L'Auberge Bourguignonne, Beaune.

7th July – Beaune to Ouistreham. Overnight stay at Le Phare, Ouistreham.

8th July – Ferry sailing from Ouistreham to Portsmouth.

Brioude

Brioude

Marseille

Marseille

Marseille

Cassis

Cassis

Cassis

Aix-en-Provence

Aix-en-Provence

Aix-en-Provence

Sunday 2nd July
Day trip to
Aix-en-Provence
a beautiful city

1990

Calvi, La Corse

Tuesday 15th May – Tuesday 22nd May.

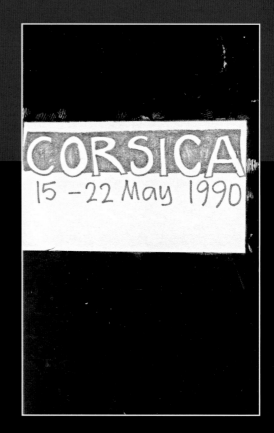

Itinerary

15th May – Flight with Dan Air from Manchester to Calvi.

15th – 22nd May – Hotel Balanea, Calvi. Package holiday with Falcon Holidays. £272.00 each.

Whilst in Calvi took two bus excursions to Cortes, the Calanques region and the villages of The Balagne region. Return train journey from Calvi to L'Ile Rousse.

Calvi

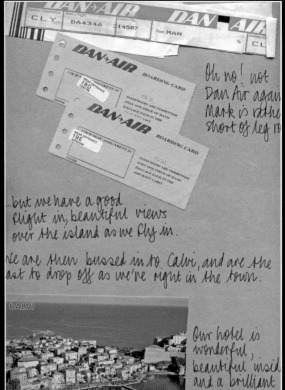

L'Isle Rousse was built by the Corsican hero Pablo Paoli who ruled Corsica in the fifteen years between the Genoan and French occupations in the seventeenth century

L'Ile Rouse

Calvi

There wasn't much to draw.

Another great Corsican rosé wine our dinner Calvi.

1991

St Aygulf, South of France

Saturday 25th May to Saturday 8th June.

Itinerary

25th May – Ferry sailing from Dover to Calais. Drive to Nuits St Georges for overnight stay at the Hotel de L'Etoile.

26th May – Nuits St Georges to Sisteron for overnight stay at the Hotel Tivoli.

27th May – Sisteron to St Aygulf where we had hired an apartment through the Agence Lombard.

28th May to 6th June – St Aygulf. Whilst in St Aygulf trips to Fréjus, St Maxime, Antibes, Cannes, Menton, Monaco, Gourdon & Grasse.

6th June – Drive from St Aygulf to Autun. Overnight stay at Hotel Saint Louis, Autun.

7th June – Drive from Autun to St Omer. Overnight stay at Le Bretagne, St Omer.

8th June – Drive from St Omer to Calais. Ferry sailing to Dover.

Sisteron

Fréjus

The artist

Menton

Sisteron

1992

South of France / Northern France

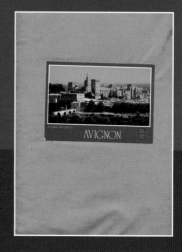

(12 day break in the south cut short by bad weather and relocation to the north) Saturday 16th May to Saturday 29th May.

Itinerary

16th May – Ferry sailing Dover to Boulogne. Drive to Vichy. Overnight stay at Camping Les Acacias, Bellerive, Vichy.

17th May – Vichy to St Flour (Lunch) to Millau to Marseillan Plage.

17th – 22nd May – Keycamp Mobile Home on site at Marseillan Plage. Whilst at Marseillan Plage trips to Marseillan, Mèze, Sète, St Guilhem le Désert, Soubes, Lodève, Montpellier, Carcassonne and Avignon. Non-stop rain for three days and with no sign of it improving initiated a decision to up sticks and drive north.

23rd May – Drive from Marseillan to Vichy (weather in Vichy glorious for last three days). Overnight stay at the campsite we had visited on the journey down.

24th May – Raining as we woke. Drive from Vichy to Rue close to the mouth of the Seine.

28th May – Quand Plage campsite. Whilst here trips to Montreuil and St Valery Sur Somme.

28th May – Quand plage to Montreuil-Sur-Mer. Overnight stay at the Le Darnetal (Hotel), Montreuil-Sur- Mer.

29th May – Montreuil-Sur-Mer to Boulogne. Ferry sailing to Dover.

Marseillan. Catherine wanted to buy this property and convert it into a studio

look at these mega cups! ↗

Grands crèmes at Séte

Avignon – Palais du Papes

Mouth of the River Somme

SATURDAY 22nd May

Oh no. The weather was still cold and wet. Knowing that the cloud was confined to the coast we decided to leave the mobile home and drove north to find the sun. Luckily we had the tent.

We went back to Vichy to the lovely campsite we'd found on our way down. The lady there said it had been sunny there all week and was forecast to continue. We got an "emplacement" in the sun. Great decision!

BRENNAND
2 pers
arrivée 23 Mai-

2 Pers x 18 = 36
1 Voiture   10
1 Place   12
               ___
               58ᶠ

S.A.R.L. CAMPING
LES ACACIAS****
Tél.: 70 32 36 22
03700 BELLERIVE
R.C. CUSSET B 341 006 545 (87 B 76)

1993

Marseillan Plage, South of France

Friday 21st May to Saturday 5th June 1993.

Itinerary

21st May – Ferry sailing from Dover to Calais. SNCF Autorail and Wagon Lits Calais to Avignon.

22nd May – Avignon. Lunch in Avignon before driving to Marseillan Plage.

22nd May – 2nd June. Keycamp Mobile Home on site at Marseillan Plage. Whilst in Marseillan trips to; Agde, Béziers, Arles, Montpellier & Aigues-Mortes.

2nd June – Drive from Marseillan Plage to St Michel de Fronsac just east of Bordeaux to stay with Catherine's cousin Juliet and her French husband Claude.

3rd June – Day trip to St Emillion.

4th June – St Michel de Fronsac to Le Havre.

5th June – Ferry sailing from Le Havre to Portsmouth.

While we waited for our train from Calais to Avignon Mark continued to listen to the cricket

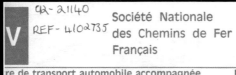

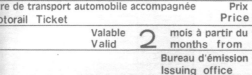

Société Nationale des Chemins de Fer Français

42-21140
REF- 4102735

re de transport automobile accompagnée ...torail Ticket

Prix Price — Forfait — FRF

Valable Valid 2 mois à partir du months from — 21/5/93

Bureau d'émission Issuing office

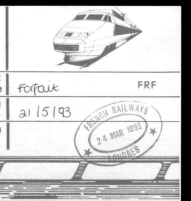

Montpellier

Had a brilliant lunch
in this restaurant. The
waiter was super. I had a warm
salad with bacon (lardons) and
croutons and we both had paupiettes
of beef in a delicious sauce. In
the middle of our meal a small
spaniel made a dash for freedom
through the restaurant with
the waiter in hot pursuit — they
were not seen for some minutes.

By the Canal du Midi.
My pastis and Mark's
Campari which he thought
might be like Noilly
Prat but wasn't!

1994

Porto Vecchio, La Corse

Sunday 15th May to Saturday 28th May.

Itinerary

15th May – Flight from Gatwick to Ajaccio. Car hire to Porto Vecchio.

15th May – 28th May – Mari di Soli Apartment Complex, nr Porto Vecchio.

Whilst here trips to Porto Vecchio, Bastia & Bonifacio.

Holiday booked through Simply Travel.

28th May – Return flight to Gatwick.

Mark is very amused by me drawing all my clothes. I find it's the only way I don't end up on holiday with nothing that goes together.

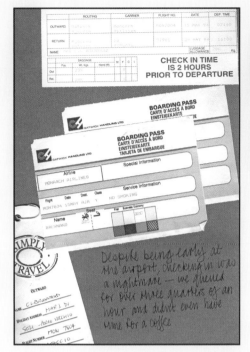

Bastia

Despite being early at the airport, checking in was a nightmare — we queued for over three quarters of an hour and didn't even have time for a coffee

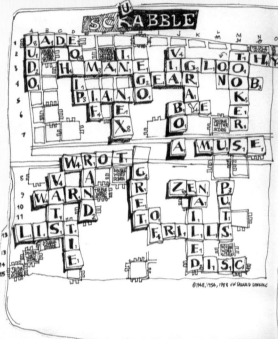

The Scrabble championship begins!

Bonifacio

Scrabble: 16th May 1994
Mari de Soli

M	C
25 37 56	10 20 34
84 94 100	48 60 74
102 132 145	85 107 122
181 199 225	146 164 205
233 243 255	237 249 255
263 270 275	268 278 280
	279

1995

Les Stes-Marie-de-la-Mer, Camargue

Sunday 4th June to Saturday 17th June.

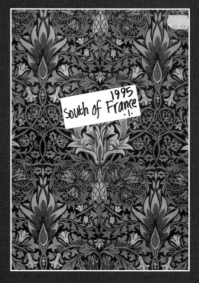

Itinerary

4th June – Folkstone to Calais using Le Shuttle. SNCF Autorail and Couchette to Avignon.

5th June – Avignon. Drive to Orange for lunch. Drive to Les Stes Marie de la Mer.

5th – 14th June. Mobile Home at Camping La Brise in Les Stes-Marie-de-la-Mer. Whilst here trips to: Aigues-Mortes, Aix-en-Provence, Les Baux de Provence, Arles, and Montpellier.

15th June – Drive from Les Stes-Marie-de-la-Mer to Vierzon. Overnight stay at B&B.

16th June – Drive from Vierzon to Fontainebleau and then Chantilly where we stay at the Hostellerie du Lys.

17th June – Chantilly to Calais. Ferry sailing to Dover.

Les Saintes Maries de la Mer – car rally

Arles

Aix-en-Provence

Cathedral of St. Saviours

We spent a wonderful
half-an-hour listening
to the organist practising
Handel and Bach. We
could see him clearly up
above us (see drawing) and
marvelled at his twinkling
feet on the pedals.

Aix-en-Provence

Les Baux de Provence

Aix-en-Provence – Red Cross Hospital

Chantilly – Musée Vivant du Cheval

Arles

BOUTIQUE VAN GOGH

1997

Cargesse, La Corse

Saturday 21st June – Saturday 28th June.

Itinerary

21st June – Flight from Gatwick to Ajaccio. Car hire to Cargesse north of Ajaccio.

21st – 28th June – Self Catering chalet at La Datura, Itylon nr to Cargesse. Whilst here day trip to Calvi.

Holiday booked through Simply Travel. Jack's first holiday abroad.

28th June – Return flight to Gatwick.

Corsica

SIMPLY
Corsica

Chiswick Gate, 598-608 Chiswick High Road,
London W4 5RT, U.K.
Telephone: 0181 747 3580
Fax: 0181 995 5346 / 0181 742 2330
Telex: 8955503 Simply G.
Email: cor@simply-travel.com

Calvi Checklist

RUCKSACK
TOWELS x 3
SUN TAN LOTION x 3
DRIVING LICENSE / PASSPORT / TRAVELLERS CHEQUES.
SWIM TRUNKS / REST OF CLOTHING.

BABY PLAY PEN - TOYS FOR J

SUN BROLLY   HandBag: cash, camera, films

CAMERA

SUNGLASSES

McLAREN BABY BUGGY.
FOOD: water, milk powder, juice
         lunch
         tea
bibs, spoons, dishes
NAPPY CHANGING KIT

Scrabble – Monday 23rd June 1997

Residence D'Itylon – Cargese, Corsica.
First time abroad with Baby J.

M	C.
6 18 36 40 54	24 39 46 52 83 91 ff
69 79 86 99 132	104 115 131 150 179 201 226
171 186 199 206 216	236 254 257 264 272 258
221 228 277	

Cargesse

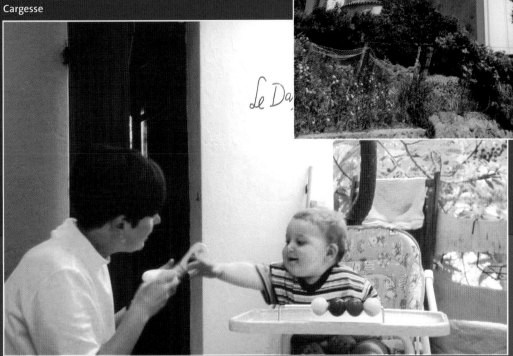

1999

Paris

Friday 20th August to Monday 23rd August.

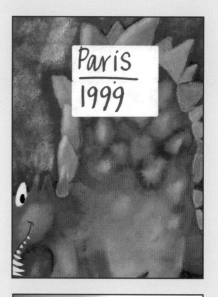

Itinerary

20th August – Flight from Glasgow to Paris Charles de Gaulle via East Midlands Airport.

20th August – Hotel Leonardo de Vinci in Parmentier District. Trip to the Sacré Cœur and Montmartre.

21st August – Place de la Madeleine, La Place de Vendôme, Le Marais, Place des Vosges, Place de l'Etoile, Arc de Triomphe, Champs Elysée, Place de la Madeleine, Parmentier.

22nd August – Place de l'Hotel de Ville, Ile de St Louis, Notre Dame Cathedral, Pont Neuf, St Germain des Prés, Eiffel Tower, Place des Invalides, Tuileries, Place de la Madeleine, La Bourse de Paris, Parmentier.

23rd August – L'Opéra & Shops (Lafayette), Place Vendôme, Café de la Paix (the place to watch the world go by).

Return flight from Charles de Gaulle Airport to Glasgow via East Midlands Airport.

Friday 20th

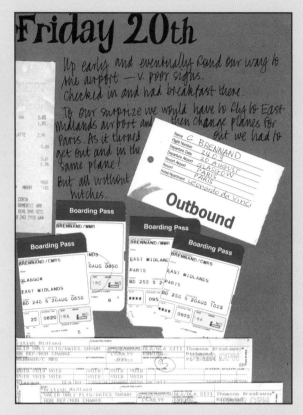

Up early and eventually found our way to the airport — v. poor signs.
Checked in and had breakfast there.

To our surprize we would have to fly to East Midlands airport and then change planes for Paris. As it turned out we had to get out and in the same plane! But all without hitches.

20th august 1999
friday

Alarm at ten to six! Up and on the road by 20 past and at airport for 6.45. Got there OK, eventually — signposting v. poor. Saw a hare within five metres while we parked the car, having a wee in the car park. Bizarre. Had to change flights at East Midlands Airport, but no problem and arrived at 12.45 French time. Caught the train to Gard du Nord and then to Republique. A bit of a trek to Hotel (Leonardo da Vinci) with bags, but soon sorted. All fine — hotel nothing special but fine.

In the afternoon we got stuck in to the tourist thing and took the Metro to Sacré-Coeur/Montmartre. The viaduct was under repair so we took the bus detour. The weather was fab, and we had a lovely time mooching about, eating pizza, climbing up the Dôme and wandering around Montmartre. Got some great painting material. Sadly in the crush on the bus detour someone stole Mark's money wallet. Luckily no credit cards or irreplaceable stuff but a pain nonetheless. I felt sorry I'd split the holiday money between us. Anyway I've got enough.

Had a good, reasonable meal in Place de la Republique and went home for an early night — writing postcards and this.

Saturday 21st

Walked to Republique. Bought two day passes to the metro. At FF48 excellent value...

21st august 1999
saturday

What a fab day. We walked our feet off then we walked more. Underground to Place de la Madeleine to see all the little shops - Fauchon, Hédiard etc - that John Lenanton recommended. Lovely and sunny and masses of great painting material - Rues Tronchet, Royale and Rivoli. Also Rue de St. Honoré, Place de la Vendôme (Ritz and Chopin). Sadly the St. Roch restaurant John recommended for lunch wasn't open but we had a good meal in Castiglione café. (escargots + steak au poivre). Après-midi Rue de Rivoli, via Louvre + Pyramid (didn't go in), Rivoli, detour round the Marais via Rue Bourg-Tibourg and afternoon tea at Mariage Frères (an upmarket Snapes + tea room) then more walking round the Marais, inc Jewish quarter (an art deco synagogue + Jewish bakeries). Then we caught the underground from the Bastille to Charles de Gaulle Etoile to watch lunatic driving at the Arch de Triomphe. Then we walked all the way down the Champs Elysée back to Rue Royale and up to Place de la Madeleine to have a drink. And caught the tube back to Republic. Walking home we had a carbonara supper at a café near our hotel, then home, diary and bed — exhausted! Four films of excellent material though in FAB weather (I got a bit burnt) so a really worthwhile day. And FUN too. Really feel we're getting to grips with Paris.

Sunday 22nd

Another wonderful sunny and hot day.

And Day Two of John's Tours!

Took Metro to Hôtel de Ville and walked along the Seine to Pont Marie. Crossed to Ile St. Louis.

Very smart area full of lovely sh... and galleries.

Wandered around along Rue St Lou...

Another fab hot sunny day. Off on John's Tour 2. Caught underground to Hôtel de Ville and then walked down to Ile St. Louis along the Seine. v. smart area full of lovely shops, galleries and other bldgs. wandered around for a bit and then stopped at a wonderful café for hot choc & grand crème respectively Café St. Pierre. The chocolate was the best EVER. A little jug of melted chocolate and big of hot milk - it made three huge cups and still milk left over, and such a lovely place too. We "did" Ile de la Cité & Notre Dame then off down Rue de Seine to St. Germain des Prés. As John had said, lots of great little shops and bars. I shall have so much wonderful painting material from this trip. We avoided the hot spots of Les Deux Magot and Café Flore and went down Rue St. Benoît to eat at Le Muniche from John's book. We didn't get far enough for his recommendations on the other side of the Jardins Luxembourg. Then we caught the tube to Tour Eiffel, walked from there to Hôtel des Invalides then tube to Place de la Concorde / Tuileries, drank at bar on Rue Royale (I had sorbet + Mark had a £6 beer!) Then walked to the Bourse and caught tube home. So much walking, we're catching up behind places we've been before already! The Tuileries is opp. Rue de Rivoli + Rue Castiglione to Place Vendôme. Not really our style - fairground stuff. When we got home it was around 8.30pm and we flopped on the bed exhausted.

Monday 23rd

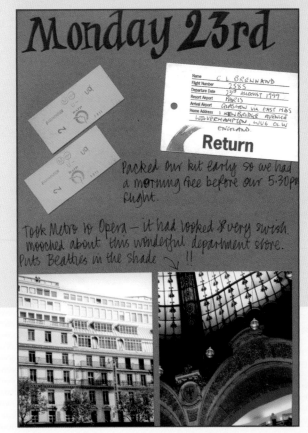

Name C L BRENNAND
Flight Number 2585
Departure Date 23rd AUGUST 1999
Resort Airport PARIS
Arrival Airport GLASGOW VIA EAST MIDS
Home Address 1 KEW BRIDGE AVENUE
WOLVERHAMPTON, WV6 OLW
ENGLAND.

Return

Packed our kit early so we had a morning free before our 5.30pm flight.

Took Metro to Opera — it had looked & very swish. mooched about this wonderful department store. Puts Beatties in the shade ↘ !!

An early night — and a good night's sleep and we were up at 8am. Quick breakfast — the continental hotels have it easy! No egg, bacon, blackpudding and haggis here! Then packed and left luggage in their room round the back of reception and off we went again! Thank goodness for my fab Hawkshead boots. They were once black suede, now dust of Paris coloured! We went to Opera - it seemed lovely - swish shops and smart bars. Went to Galleries Lafayette, an AMAZING department store - all the big names in perfume and clothes and a fab atrium with ornulue-style balconies. We wandered around and I bought a wonderful Max Mara grey wool skirt. Lovely ankle length and v. slimming - flat at the top and then full at the bottom, excellent for autumn/winter with boots, my Bergdf Goodman tights and black sweater. We had lunch at Café des Paix, citron pressé pour moi + Orangina also two baguettes = £15.00. This upsets Mark. But I think, so what. We got great value (£42.00) at Le Muniche yesterday for three courses, ½ bottle of Côtes de Provence + aperitifs. Then it was travelling time. BIG BAGGAGE. Everytime we do this we talk about luggage with wheels. Then we forget. Tube to Gare du Nord, train to Airport CDG, bus to terminal 1, dump luggage. Nearly buy wine as gifts - can't buy duty free in EU now. Buy Fredaud tea and coffee and chocolate instead. Am writing at Gate's — we were 1½ hrs early. Caught flight — all went smoothly + a lovely evening drive across from Station to Newton Stewart thru Galloway Forest. All well at base. Boys in bed and no rain all week. Dad said " It's v. wearying, isn't it." !!

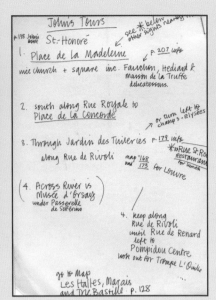

John's Tours

p.145 John's Tour

St. Honoré ← see * below other sights nearby

1. Place de la Madeleine → p.207 info
nice church + square inc. Fauchon, Hediard & Maison de la Truffe delicatessens.

2. south along Rue Royale to Place de la Concorde → or turn left to Champs-Elysées

3. Through Jardin des Tuileries p.179 info
along Rue de Rivoli map '168 and '173 for Louvre
* Rue St. Roch Restaurants for lunch

4. Across River is Musée d'Orsay under Passerelle de Solférino

4. keep along Rue de Rivoli until Rue de Renard left to Pompidou Centre look out for Trompe L'Oeile

go to Map
Les Halles, Marais and The Bastille p.128

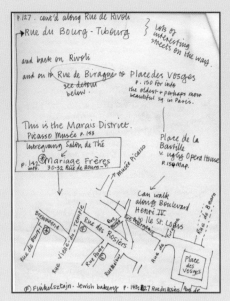

p.127 . cont'd along Rue de Rivoli

→ Rue du Bourg - Tibourg } Lots of interesting streets on the way.

and back on Rivoli

and on to Rue de Birague to Place des Vosges p.150 for info
see detour below. the oldest + perhaps most beautiful sq. in Paris.

This is the Marais District.
Picasso Musée p.143
Intriguing Salon de Thé
p.142 * Mariage Frères
info. 30-32 Rue de Bourg-T.

Place de la Bastille
v. ugly Opera House p.154 Map.

Can walk along Boulevard Henri IV. Ile St. Louis

[map with streets: Brocanterie, Rue de Bourg-T, Rue Vieille du Temple, Rue des Rosiers, Rue Payen, Rue Ferdinand, Rue St-Bernard, Rue de Bourg, Ile de B, Place des Vosges, Musée Picasso]

(F) Finkelsztajn. Jewish bakery. p.143: 27 Rue des Rosiers. Rue de

---

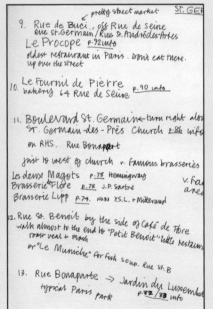

ST. GER

9. Rue de Buci . off Rue de Seine ← pretty street market
Rue St. Germain / Rue St. André des Arts
Le Procope p.92 info
oldest restaurant in Paris. Don't eat there. up over the street

10. Le Fournil de Pierre p.90 info
bakery 64 Rue de Seine

11. Boulevard St. Germain ← turn right along
St. Germain-des-Près Church p.86 info
on RHS. Rue Bonaparte
just to west of church v. famous brasseries
Les deux Magots p.78 Hemingway
Brasserie Flore p.78 J.P. Sartre
Brasserie Lipp p.74. No33 X.S.L. + Mitterand
v. fa and

12. Rue St. Benoît by the side of Café de Flore
walk almost to the end to "Petit Benoit" little restaurant
roast veal + mash
or "Le Muniche" for fish soup. Rue St. B

13. Rue Bonaparte → Jardin du Luxembourg
typical Paris park p.82 / 83 info

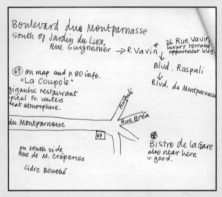

Boulevard du Montparnasse
south of Jardin du Lux,
Rue Guynemer → R. Vavin
* 26 Rue Vavin luxury terraced apartment bldg.

(69) on map and p.80 info.
"La Coupole"
gigantic restaurant typical Fr. waiters great atmosphere.

Blvd. Raspail
Blvd. du Montparnasse

du Montparnasse
Rue Bréa
[69]
Raspail

on south side
Rue de M. Crêperies
Cidre Bouché

* Bistro de la Gare also near here. v. good.

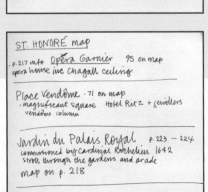

ST. HONORÉ map

p.217 info. Opéra Garnier 95 on map
opera house inc. Chagall ceiling

Place Vendôme · 71 on map
· magnificent square Hotel Ritz + jewellers
vendôme column

Jardin du Palais Royal p.223 - 224
commissioned by Cardinal Richelieu 1642
stroll through the gardens and arade
map on p. 218

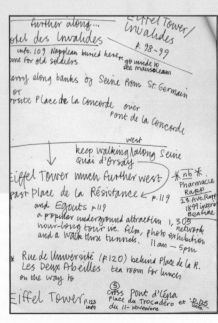

further along... Eiffel Tower / Invalides p.98-99

Hotel des Invalides
info. 109 Napolean buried here → go inside to see mausoleum
Home for old soldiers

Carry along banks of Seine from St. Germain
or
opposite Place de la Concorde over Pont de la Concorde

west
keep walking along Seine Quai d'Orsay

Eiffel Tower much further west) * nb *
past Place de la Résistance ← p.119
Pharmacie Rapp 23 Ave. Rapp 1899 interior Beaune
and Egouts p.119
a popular underground attraction 1,305 network
hour-long tour inc. film, photo exhibition
and a walk thru tunnels. 11am - 5pm

* Rue de Université (p.120) behind Place de la R.
Les Deux Abeilles tea room for lunch
on the way to

Eiffel Tower p.123 info (5) cross Pont d'Iéna p.125 info
Place du Trocadéro et du 11- Novembre

2004

Montpellier

Saturday 14th – Friday 20th February 2004.

Itinerary

14th February – Flight from Heathrow Airport to Montpellier via Charles de Gaulle.

14th – 20th February – Apartment in Montpellier. Whilst there trips to Nîmes and Palavas.

20th February – Return flight from Montpellier to Heathrow via Charles de Gaulle. Missed connecting flight at Charles de Gaulle due to Air Traffic Controllers strike which had delayed our departure from Montpellier.

Montpellier February 2004

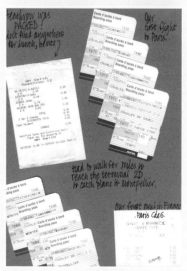

Friday 14th Feb

Left home around 11:15 and arrived at "Park 4 Less" with no trouble.

Managed to pack everything into two cases. One with wheels and the other on my old trolley...

Heathrow was PACKED! Couldn't find anywhere for lunch, hence :)

Our first flight to Paris.

Had to walk for miles to reach the terminal 2D to catch plane to Montpellier.

Our first meal in France. Paris CdG.

So impressed with the Metro
(BOYS buy cars on the way home)

Montpellier

Nîmes

Friday 20th
Interesting journey home!
Got up really early to wash bedding from boys' bed, and our taxi driver turned up at 7.30 am. Had a great chat with h... all a... the Roma...

breakfast at airport

OK so far

CABINE

Sadly Mlle Chauroud's hopes of the st/ve ending were misplaced

CAFE SELECT
MONTPELLIER

TOTAL   18.40

Didn't leave Montpellier 'til gone 11am

Had a nightmare trying to find the other terminal and eventually got there on a bus which took the long way round.

Eventually got to our Gate with five minutes to spare, but they wouldn't let us fly.

CHRONOLOGICAL LIST OF PAINTINGS AND, WHERE KNOWN, LINE DRAWINGS

All pictures are in private collections unless stated. Dimensions, where known, are given in centimetres, height before width.

1.   Yellow Door, Le Castellet, Provence (September 1987) Pge 93
2.   Tanner's Houses, Entraygues-sur-Truyère, Massif Central (November 1987) Pge 75
3.   The Red Cross Hospital, Aix-en-Provence (April 1989) Pge 3
4.   Looking down a street in St Tropez. 38 × 51cm. Watercolour and wax resist (May 1989) Pge 94
5.   Street in Brioude, Central France. Watercolour and wax resist (January 1990) Pge 75
6.   Corner of a street, Aix-en-Provence. 48 × 36cm. Watercolour and wax resist (March 1990) Pge 5
7.   A street in Cyreste, Provence. 46 × 36cm. Watercolour and wax resist (March 1990) Pge 95
8.   Backstreets of Marseille. 49 × 34cm. Watercolour and wax resist (March 1990) Pge 96
9.   Door in Brioude, Central France. 18 × 22cm. Watercolour and wax resist (July 1990) Pge 76
10. Door in Brioude, Central France. 18 × 22cm. Watercolour and wax resist (August 1990) Pge 76
11. Door in Brioude, Central France. 18 × 22cm. Watercolour and wax resist (November 1990) Pge 76
12. Door in Brioude, Central France. 22 × 18cm. Watercolour and wax resist (December 1990) Pge 76
13. Façade, Aix-en-Provence. 76 × 56cm. Watercolour and wax resist (December 1990) Accepted for 1991 exhibition of Royal Institute of Painters in Watercolours. The winner of the 1991 Young Painters in Watercolours Award. (Sponsored by Winsor & Newton). Pge 4
14. Villa St Pierre, Cannes, Cote D'Azur. 70 × 30cm. Watercolour (September 1991) Pge 96
15. The Marine Museum II, Orange and Blue, Grasse, Cote D'Azur. 54 × 36cm. (March 1993) *plus line drawing* Pge 97
16. Menton Church. 65 × 54cm. Watercolour (April 1993) Pge 97
17. Cercle Fragonard, Grasse. 36 × 54cm. Watercolour (April 1993) Pge 98
18. Plane Tree, Cercle Fragonard, Grasse. 36 × 54cm. Watercolour (April 1993) Pge 98
19. No 37, Avignon Door. 35 × 26cm. Watercolour (April 1993) Pge 98
20. No 92, Fréjus Door, Cote D'Azur. 35 × 26cm. Watercolour (April 1993) Pge 98
21. Bunting in Fréjus, Cote D'Azur. 68 × 33cm. Watercolour (April 1993) Pge 99
22. Palm Tree, Sanary, Cote D'Azur. 68 × 28.5cm. Watercolour (May 1993) Pge 99
23. Door at No 24, Fayence, Gulf D'Estoril. 39 × 23cm. Watercolour and wax resist (May 1993) Pge 100
24. Door at No 21, Nuits-St-Georges, Bourgogne. 39 × 23cm. Watercolour (May 1993) Pge 77
25. Rue Gabriel Péri, Sète. 30.5 × 21cm. Watercolour. (May 1993) Pge 83
26. Hotel du Palais, Montpellier. 30.5 × 21cm. Watercolour (May 1993) Pge 34
27. Saint in a Niche, Avignon. 36 × 54cm. (May 1993) Pge 100
28. Place du Forum, Arles. 36 × 54cm. (June 1994) Pge 47
29. Ivy on a house in Arles. 37 × 51cm. Watercolour and wax resist (June 1994) Pge 47
30. Gold Façade, Avignon. 21 × 31cm. Watercolour and wax resist (August 1994) Pge 101
31. Ornamental Ironwork, Avignon. 21 × 31cm. Watercolour and wax resist (August 1994) Pge 101
32. Hotel du Forum, Arles. 31 × 21cm. Watercolour and wax resist (August 1994) Pge 48

33. Place du Forum, Arles. 31 × 21cm. Watercolour and wax resist (August 1994) Pge 48

34. Leaping Goat Statue, Chantilly Chateau. 31 × 21cm. Watercolour and wax resist (July 1995) Pge 77

35. Bronze Head, Chantilly Chateau. 31 × 21cm. Watercolour and wax resist (July 1995) *plus line drawing* Pge 78

36. Green Door at Number 1, Chantilly. 36 × 55cm. Watercolour and wax resist (August 1995) Pge 78

37. Terracotta Pots outside the Montpellier Chamber of Commerce. 54 × 36cm. (September 1995) Pge 33

38. Doorway with Stone Vases, Aix-en-Provence. 30.5 × 54.5cm. Watercolour, wax resist and tissue (January 1996) Pge 5

39. Ornate Doorway in Gold & Blue, Aix-en-Provence. 36.5 × 50cm. Watercolour and wax resist (January 1996) Pge 6

40. Blue Shutters, Place de Palmiers, Aix-en-Provence. 34 × 54cm. (January 1996) Pge 6

41. Green Lantern, Aix-en-Provence. 36 × 54cm. (January 1996) Pge 7

42. Three Stone Faces, Aix-en-Provence. 36 × 54cm. (January 1996) Pge 7

43. Statue on Corner of Rue Thiers, Aix-en-Provence. 21 × 30.5cm. (February 1996) Pge 8

44. Corner of Rue Aude, Aix-en-Provence. 30 × 23cm. (February 1996) *plus line drawing* Pge 9

45. Number 2 Place des Palmiers, Aix-en-Provence. 76 × 40cm. (February 1996) Pge 8

46. Corner of a courtyard, Aix-en-Provence. 31.5 × 21cm. (February 1996) Pge 9

47. Three Stone Faces at Number 10, Aix-en-Provence. 76 × 40cm. (February 1996) Pge 10

48. Boutiques on Cours Mirabeau, Aix-en-Provence. 21 × 31.5cm. (February 1996) Pge 10

49. Lantern at Number 10, Aix-en-Provence. 76 × 40cm. (February 1996) Pge 10

50. Gold Corinthian Columns, Cours Mirabeau, Aix-en-Provence. 21 × 31.5cm. (February 1996) Pge 11

51. Green Shutters at No 7, Aix-en-Provence. 76 × 40cm. (February 1996) Pge 12

52. Green Shutters at No 9, Aix-en-Provence. 32.5 × 21cm. (February 1996) Pge 11

53. Ornate Doorway. Place des Palmiers, Aix-en-Provence. 36 × 54cm. (February 1996) Pge 13

54. No 21, Cours Mirabeau, Aix-en-Provence. 21 × 30cm. (February 1996) Pge 14

55. Stone Vases at No 40, Aix-en-Provence. 69 × 35cm. (March 1996) Pge 14

56. Green Door at No 18, Aix-en-Provence. 74 × 35cm. (March 1996) Pge 14

57. Rue Thiers, Aix-en-Provence. 36 × 54cm. (April 1996) Pge 15

58. The Architect's House at No 15, Aigues-Mortes. 36 × 54cm. (April 1996) Pge 65

59. No 41, Aigues-Mortes. 54 × 36cm. (April 1996) Pge 66

60. La Boutique Française, Aix-en-Provence. 36 × 54cm. (May 1996) Pge 15

61. The Cathedral, Aix-en-Provence. 36 × 51cm. (May 1996) Pge 16

62. Hotel de Ville, Aigues-Mortes. 54 × 36cm. (May 1996) Pge 66

63. No 35, Aigues-Mortes. 54 × 36cm. (May 1996) Pge 66

64. Classical Style Window, Orange. 31.5 × 22.5cm. (June 1996) *plus line drawing* Pge 102

65. Green Shutters, Montpellier. 22.5 × 31.5cm. (June 1996) Pge 34

66. Green Balconies, Montpellier. 22.5 × 31.5cm. (June 1996) Pge 35

67. Blue shutters, gold wall, Orange. 31.5 × 22.5cm. (June 1996) Pge 102

68. Rue Sallier, Aix-en-Provence. 37.5 × 27.5cm. (June 1996) Pge 16

69. Number 15, Aix-en-Provence. 31.5 × 22.5cm. (June 1996) Pge 17

70. Green Shutters at Rue Aude, Aix-en-Provence. 38 × 28cm. (June 1996) Pge 17

71. Salle Molière, Montpellier. 74 × 35cm. (August 1996) Pge 33

72. Crimson Shutters, Orange. 36 × 36cm. (January 1997) Pge 103

73. Gold Wall, Rond Point des Arènes, Arles. 54 × 36cm. (January 1997) Pge 49

118. Le Monde. 43 × 30cm. Watercolour, wax resist and collage (November 1999) Pge 79

119. Notre Dame, Paris. Watercolour and wax resist (1999) Pge 119

120. Fauchon, place de la Madeleine, Paris. 34 × 36cm. Watercolour and collage. (November 1999). Exhibited at the RI Annual Exhibition 2000. Pge 120

121. Hediard, Place de la Madeleine, Paris. 34 × 36cm. Watercolour and collage (November 1999). Exhibited at the RI Annual Exhibition 2000. Pge 120

122. Christofle, Place de la Vendôme, Paris. 34 × 36cm. Watercolour and collage (November 1999). Exhibited at the RI Annual Exhibition 2000. Pge 120

123. Biberon, Rue St Honore, Paris. 36 × 54cm. Watercolour and collage (November 1999). Exhibited at the RI Annual Exhibition 2000. Pge 121

124. Cartier, Place de la Vendôme, Paris. 34 × 36cm. Watercolour and collage (December 1999). Exhibited at the RI Annual Exhibition 2000. Pge 122

125. Cristal Lalique, Rue de Rivoli, Paris. 34 × 36cm. Watercolour, collage and wax resist. (December 1999) Exhibited at the RI Annual Exhibition 2000. Pge 125

126. Institut de Beauté Guerlain, Champs Elysées, Paris. 34 × 36cm. Watercolour, collage and wax resist (December 1999) Pge 125

127. Port Royal Chocolatier, Rue de Rivoli, Paris. 25.5 × 27cm. Watercolour and collage (January 2000)Pge 124

128. Chanel, Rue Royale, Paris. 25.5 × 27cm. Watercolour and collage (January 2000) Pge 124

129. Cerutti 1881, Rue Royale, Paris. 54 × 36cm. Watercolour and collage (January 2000) Pge 125

130. Le Gastelier Salon de Thé, Montmartre, Paris. 36 × 54cm. Watercolour and collage (February 2000) Pge 126

131. Arcades des Champs Elysées, Paris. 54 × 36cm. Watercolour and collage (February 2000) Pge 126

132. Galeries Félix Haloux, Ile St Louis, Paris. 36 × 54cm. Watercolour and collage (February 2000) Pge 127

133. Boulangerie St Louis, Ile St Louis, Paris. 54 × 36cm. Watercolour and collage (February 2000) Pge 127

134. Boulangerie L. Chevalier, Montmartre, Paris. 70 × 34cm. Watercolour (February 2000) *plus line drawing* Pge 128

135. Vins Fins – Fromages, Rue Tardieu, Montmartre. 70 × 34cm. Watercolour (February 2000) Pge 128

136. Les Deux Margots, St Germain des Prés, Paris. 54 × 36. Watercolour and collage (February 2000) Pge 129

137. Le Petit Zinc Restaurant, St Germain des Prés, Paris. 36 × 54cm. (February 2000) *plus line drawing* Pge 129

138. Café de Flore, St Germain des Prés, Paris. 54 × 36cm. Watercolour and collage (February 2000) Pge 130

139. Evening light at Fauchon, Place de la Madeleine, Paris. 74 × 28cm. (February 2000) Pge 130

140. Restaurant Le Consulat, Montmartre, Paris. 54 × 36cm. Watercolour and collage (February 2000) *plus line drawing* Pge 131

141. Guerlain, Rue Tronchet, Paris. 75 × 56cm. Watercolour and collage (April 2000) *plus line drawing* Pge 131

142. Devernois, Rue Tronchet, Paris. 75 × 38cm. Watercolour and collage (April 2000) *plus line drawing* Pge 134

143. Gucci, Place de Vendôme, Paris. 57 × 37cm. Watercolour and collage (April 2000) Pge 134

144. Epicerie de la Tour, Tour Eiffel, Paris. 34 × 36cm. Watercolour and collage (May 2000) *plus line drawing* Pge 135

145. Jo Goldenberg Delicatessen, Rue Ferdinand Duval, Le Marais, Paris. 34 × 36cm. Watercolour and collage (May 2000) *plus line drawing* Pge 135

146. Boucheron, Place Vendôme, Paris. 36 × 54cm. Watercolour and collage (May 2000) Pge 136

147. Red Crates outside Epicerie de la Tour, Eiffel Tower, Paris. 18 × 18cm. Watercolour and collage (May 2000) Pge 136

148. The Ritz, Place Vendôme, Paris. 75 × 40cm. Watercolour and collage (May 2000) Pge 137

149. Cartier, Place Vendôme, Paris. 75 × 40cm. Watercolour and collage (June 2000) Pge 137

150. Hotel Vendôme, Place Vendôme, Paris. 75 × 40cm. Watercolour and collage (July 2000) Pge 138

151. Three Stone Heads. Bulgari, Place Vendôme, Paris. 34 × 36cm. Watercolour and collage (July 2000) Pge 138

152. Biberon & Fils, 334 Rue St Honore, Paris. 34 × 36cm. Watercolour and collage (July 2000)*plus line drawing* Pge 139

153. Shadow of Street Lamp, Cristal Lalique, Rue de Rivoli, Paris. 36 × 34cm. Watercolour and collage (July 2000) Pge 140

154. Salon de Thé, An Lys d'Argent, Ile St Louis, Paris. 36 × 34cm. Watercolour and collage (July 2000) Pge 140

155. Conifers outside Cristofle, Place Vendôme, Paris. 36 × 34cm. Watercolour and collage (July 2000) Pge 141

156. Aux Tortues, Boulangerie, Rue Tronchet, Paris, 36 × 34cm. Watercolour and collage (August 2000) Pge 141

157. Evening Light, Institut de Beauté Guerlain, Champs Elysées, Paris. 36 × 34cm. (August 2000) Pge 142

158. Gold Lantern, Cristal Lalique, Rue de Rivoli, Paris. 34 × 36cm. (September 2000) Pge 142

159. Devernois, Rue Tronchet, Paris. 33 × 65cm. Watercolour and collage (November 2000) Pge 143

160. Guerlain Rue Tronchet, Paris. 36 × 54cm. Watercolour and collage (November 2000) Pge 143

161. Chopin's House (Chaumet) 12 Place Vendôme, Paris. 75 × 34.5cm. (March 2001) Pge 144

162. Marie Curie's House, 36 Quai D'Orléans, Ile St Louis, Paris. 30 × 36cm. Watercolour and collage. (May 2001) Pge 144

163. Looking up at Cartier, Place Vendôme, Paris. 74 × 30cm. Watercolour and collage. (May 2001) Pge 145

164. Pâtisserie Capucines, Rue de Seze, L'Opéra, Paris. 36 × 26cm. Watercolour, Indian ink & wax resist. (May 2001) Pge 146

165. Ministère de la Justice, Place Vendôme, Paris. 36 × 26cm. Watercolour, Indian ink & wax resist. (May 2001) Pge 146

166. Café Madeleine, Place de la Madeleine, Paris. 36 × 26cm. Watercolour, Indian ink & wax resist. (May 2001) Pge 147

167. Marionnaud, Rue des Maturins, Paris. 36 × 26cm. Watercolour, Indian ink & wax resist. (May 2001) Pge 146

168. Marquise de Sevigne Chocolatier, Place de la Madeleine, Paris. 36 × 26cm. Watercolour, Indian ink & wax resist (May 2001) Pge 147

169. Café de la Paix, Place L'Opéra, Paris. 36 × 26cm. Watercolour, Indian ink & wax resist. (May 2001) Pge 146

170. Plane tree outside Guerlain, Champs Elysées, Paris. 54 × 36cm. Watercolour and collage. (August 2001) Pge 148

171. Le Tardieu Café, Montmartre, Paris. 33 × 22cm. Watercolour, Indian ink & wax resist. (April 2002) Pge 148

172. Le Gastelier, Salon de Thé, Montmartre, Paris. 36.5 × 23.5cm. Watercolour, Indian ink & wax resist. (April 2002) Pge 149

173. Quai d'Orléans, Ile de Paris, Paris. 26 x65cm. Watercolour and collage. (April 2002) Pge 149

174. Ornate Balcony, Cours Mirabeau, Aix-en-Provence. 39 × 25cm. Watercolour and collage. (December 2003) Pge 24

175. Société Générale, 16 Cours Mirabeau, Aix-en-Provence. 39 × 25cm. Watercolour and collage. (December 2003) Pge 24

176. Ornate Door, 14 Cours Mirabeau, Aix-en-Provence. 39 × 25cm. Watercolour and collage. (December 2003) Pge 24

177. Green Door, Cours Mirabeau, Aix-en-Provence. 39 × 25cm. Watercolour and collage. (December 2003) Pge 24

178. Bibliothèque pour tous, 19 Rue Cardinale, Aix-en-Provence. 45 × 20cm. Watercolour and collage. (January 2004) Pge 25

179. Green Door & Shutters at No 27, Aix-en-Provence. 45 × 20cm. Watercolour and collage. (January 2004) Pge 25

180. Christian Lacroix, Aix-en-Provence. 45 × 20cm. Watercolour and collage. (January 2004) *plus line drawing* Pge 26

181. Red Geraniums at No 33, Aix-en-Provence. 27 × 27cm. Watercolour and collage. (January 2004) Pge 27

182. Geraniums on a balcony, Aix-en-Provence. 21.5 × 21.5cm. Watercolour and collage (January 2004) Pge 27

183. Monoprix, Aix-en-Provence. 20.5 × 20.5cm. Watercolour and collage. (January 2004) Pge 27

184. Arched Doorway at No 35, Aix-en-Provence. 45 × 20cm. Watercolour and collage (January 2004) *plus line drawing* Pge 28

185. La Table Aixoise Restaurant, Aix-en-Provence. 50 × 33cm. Watercolour, Indian ink & wax resist (January 2004) *plus line drawing* Pge 29

186. Reflection of the Arena, Nîmes. 34 × 36cm. Watercolour and collage (April 2004) *plus line drawing* Pge 86

187. Reflection of the Gaumont, Place de la Comédie, Montpellier. 29 × 29cm. Watercolour and collage. (May 2004) *plus line drawing* Pge 40

188. Palais Nîmes, Reflection of the Amphitheatre, Nîmes. 36 × 34cm. Watercolour tissue and collage. (May 2004) Pge 87

189. Banque NSMD, Rue Foch, Montpellier. 36 × 34cm. Watercolour and collage. (May 2004) Pge 40

190. Le Café Bourse, Nîmes. 36 × 34cm. Watercolour with bodycolour and tissue collage. (May 2004) Pge 87

191. Reflection of the Maison Carrée, Nîmes. 34 × 36cm. Watercolour, tissue and collage (June 2004) *plus line drawing* Pge 88

192. Galerie Alexander Fleur, Rue Jean Jacques Rousseau, Montpellier. 44 × 26cm. Watercolour body-colour with tissue collage (June 2004) *plus line drawing* Pge 41

193. The Corner of Rue Foch and Rue D'Albisson, Montpellier. 36 × 54cm. Watercolour and tissue collage (June 2004) *plus line drawing* Pge 42

194. Pâtisserie Valgalier, Rue du Faubourg St Jaumes, Montpellier. 27.5 × 21.5cm. (June 2004) *plus line drawing* Pge 43

195. Restaurant le Phénix, Arles. 49.5 × 28.5cm. Watercolour and tissue collage (June 2004) Pge 60

196. Balcony at No 23, Aigues-Mortes. 37 × 37cm. Watercolour and tissue collage (June 2004) Pge 71

197. Villa Romana, Arles. 65 × 36cm. (June 2004) Pge 61

CATHERINE BRENNAND RI

1961–2006

"There are many artists who find inspiration for their work in a variety of sources and themes and there are others for whom there need only be one." So wrote Simon Fenwick in his Obituary published in The Independent on 3rd August 2006. "Catherine Brennand's passion was buildings; *'I cannot ever imagine becoming bored with painting buildings. There are so many architectural styles and every place has its own flavour. Also I am particularly interested in the use of light and shadows, the buildings surface is constantly changing. A good light can make the most mundane of buildings come alive.'*"

Inspired by the work of John Piper, Graham Sutherland and Mark Rothko, Catherine Brennand began painting in 1987. In 1991 her painting "Facade; Aix-en-Provence" won the Young Painter in Watercolour Award (Sponsored by Winsor and Newton) at the Annual Exhibition of Royal Institute of Painters in Watercolour. The following year she became a full member of the Institute (RI) and from 2001 served on its Council.

Diagnosed with breast cancer in July 2002, she continued to paint full time through two courses of chemotherapy before dying (aged 44) on 1st May 2006.

During her short life Catherine completed over 900 works of predominantly architectural subjects in Great Britain, France, Italy, the USA, Israel, Spain and Malta. She was regularly commissioned by both individuals and companies to paint favoured subjects, principally private residences and commercial properties.

Catherine Brennand's France is the first in a series of books celebrating her work.